MW01519006

Toys Crochet

Step By Step Guide Crochet Animals, Dolls, and Other Playthings for Kids

Copyright © 2020

All rights reserved.

DEDICATION

Contents

Buttercup Bear

Very easy to make - but she looks so cute. Who could resist her?

To make Buttercup Bear I used:

Yellow double knitting yarn – about 55g

3mm crochet hook

Notions – toy stuffing, oddments of black yarn, pink ribbon.

PATTERN

(English terms used)dc (English) = sc (American)

Finished size – approximately 28 cm (11 inches) tall from top to toes.

Body

With yellow and 3 mm hook make 2 chain.

1st round: 6 dc (US = sc) into 2nd chain from hook. Join with a slip st into 1st dc.

2nd round: 1 ch, 2 dc into same stitch as chain, [2 dc into next dc] 5 times. Sl st into 1st dc. (12 dc)

3rd round: 1 ch, 2 dc into same stitch as chain, 1 dc into next dc, [2 dc into next dc, 1 dc into next dc] 5 times. Sl st into 1st dc. (18 dc)

4th round: 1 ch, 2 dc into same stitch as chain, 1 dc into next 2 dc, [2 dc into next dc, 1 dc into next 2 dc] 5 times. Sl st into 1st dc. (24 dc)

5th round: 1 ch, 2 dc into same stitch as chain, 1 dc into next 3 dc, [2 dc into next dc, 1 dc into next 3 dc] 5 times. Sl st into 1st dc. (30 dc)

2

6th round: 1 ch, 2 dc into same stitch as chain, 1 dc into next 4 dc, [2 dc into next dc, 1 dc into next 4 dc] 5 times. Sl st into 1st dc. (36 dc)

7th round: 1 ch, 2 dc into same stitch as chain, 1 dc into next 5 dc, [2 dc into next dc, 1 dc into next 5 dc] 5 times. Sl st into 1st dc. (42 dc)

8th round: 1 ch, 2 dc into same stitch as chain, 1 dc into next 6 dc, [2 dc into next dc, 1 dc into next 6 dc] 5 times. Sl st into 1st dc. (48 dc)

9th round: 1 ch, 1 dc into each stitch to end, sl st into first dc.

10th round: 1 ch, 2 dc into same stitch as chain, 1 dc into next 7 dc, [2 dc into next dc, 1 dc into next 7 dc] 5 times. Sl st into 1st dc. (54 dc)

11th round: 1 ch, 1 dc into each stitch to end, sl st into first dc.

12th round: 1 ch, 2 dc into same stitch as chain, 1 dc into next 8 dc, [2 dc into next dc, 1 dc into next 8 dc] 5 times. Sl st into 1st dc. (60 dc)

13th – 18th rounds: 1 ch, 1 dc into each stitch to end, sl st into first dc.

19th round: 1 ch, [dc2tog, 1 dc into next 8 dc] 6 times. Sl st into 1st dc. (54 dc)

20th – 21st rounds: 1 ch, 1 dc into each stitch to end, sl st into first dc.

22nd round: 1 ch, [dc2tog, 1 dc into next 7 dc] 6 times. Sl st into 1st dc. (48 dc)

23rd – 24th rounds: 1 ch, 1 dc into each stitch to end, sl st into first dc.

25th round: 1 ch, [dc2tog, 1 dc into next 6 dc] 6 times. Sl st into 1st dc. (42 dc)

26th round: 1 ch, 1 dc into each stitch to end, sl st into first dc.

27th round: 1 ch, [dc2tog, 1 dc into next 5 dc] 6 times. Sl st into 1st dc. (36 dc)

28th round: 1 ch, 1 dc into each stitch to end, sl st into first dc.

29th round: 1 ch, [dc2tog, 1 dc into next 4 dc] 6 times. Sl st into 1st dc. (30 dc)

30th round: 1 ch, 1 dc into each stitch to end, sl st into first dc.

31st round: 1 ch, [dc2tog, 1 dc into next 3 dc] 6 times. Sl st into 1st dc. (24 dc)

32nd round: 1 ch, 1 dc into each stitch to end, sl st into first dc.

33rd round: 1 ch, [dc2tog, 1 dc into next 2 dc] 6 times. Sl st into 1st dc. (18 dc)

34th round: 1 ch, 1 dc into each stitch to end, sl st into first dc.

Fasten off and stuff body. Do not close neck opening.

Head

With yellow and 3 mm hook make 2 chain.

1st round: 6 dc into 2nd chain from hook. Join with a slip st into 1st dc.

2nd round: 1 ch, 2 dc into same stitch as chain, [2 dc into next dc] 5 times. Sl st into 1st dc. (12 dc)

3rd round: 1 ch, 2 dc into same stitch as chain, 1 dc into next 3 dc, [2 dc into next dc, 1dc into next 3 dc] 2 times. Sl st into 1st dc. (15 dc)

4th round: 1 ch, 2 dc into same stitch as chain, 1 dc into next 4 dc, [2 dc into next dc, 1 dc into next 4 dc] 2 times. Sl st into 1st dc. (18 dc)

5th round: 1 ch, 2 dc into same stitch as chain, 1 dc into next 5 dc, [2 dc into next dc, 1 dc into next 5 dc] 2 times. Sl st into 1st dc. (21 dc)

6th round: 1 ch, 2 dc into same stitch as chain, 1 dc into next 6 dc, [2 dc into next dc, 1 dc into next 6 dc] 2 times. Sl st into 1st dc. (24 dc)

7th round: 1 ch, 1 dc into each stitch to end, sl st into first dc.

8th round: 1 ch, 2 dc into same stitch as chain, 1 dc into next 3 dc, [2 dc into next dc, 1 dc into next 3 dc] 5 times. Sl st into 1st dc. (30 dc)

9th round: 1 ch, 2 dc into same stitch as chain, 1 dc into next 4 dc, [2 dc into next dc, 1 dc into next 4 dc] 5 times. Sl st into 1st dc. (36 dc)

10th round: 1 ch, 2 dc into same stitch as chain, 1 dc into next 5 dc, [2 dc into next dc, 1 dc into next 5 dc] 5 times. Sl st into 1st dc. (42 dc)

11th round: 1 ch, 2 dc into same stitch as chain, 1 dc into next 6 dc, [2 dc into next dc, 1 dc into next 6 dc] 5 times. Sl st into 1st dc. (48 dc)

12th round: 1 ch, 1 dc into each stitch to end, sl st into first dc.

13th round: 1 ch, 2 dc into same stitch as chain, 1 dc into next 7 dc, [2 dc into next dc, 1 dc into next 7 dc] 5 times. Sl st into 1st dc. (54 dc)

14th – 16th rounds: 1 ch, 1 dc into each stitch to end, sl st into first dc.

17th round: 1 ch, [dc2tog, 1 dc into next 7 dc] 6 times. Sl st into 1st dc. (48 dc)

18th round: 1 ch, 1 dc into each stitch to end, sl st into first dc.

19th round: 1 ch, [dc2tog, 1 dc into next 6 dc] 6 times. Sl st into 1st dc. (42 dc)

20th round: 1 ch, 1 dc into each stitch to end, sl st into first dc.

21st round: 1 ch, [dc2tog, 1 dc into next 5 dc] 6 times. Sl st into 1st dc. (36 dc)

22nd round: 1 ch, 1 dc into each stitch to end, sl st into first dc.

23rd round: 1 ch, [dc2tog, 1 dc into next 4 dc] 6 times. Sl st into 1st dc. (30 dc)

24th round: 1 ch, 1 dc into each stitch to end, sl st into first dc.

25th round: 1 ch, [dc2tog, 1 dc into next 3 dc] 6 times. Sl st into 1st dc. (24 dc)

26th round: 1 ch, [dc2tog, 1 dc into next 2 dc] 6 times. Sl st into 1st dc. (18 dc)

27th round: 1 ch, [dc2tog, 1 dc into next 1 dc] 6 times. Sl st into 1st

dc. (12 dc)

Stuff head at this point.

28th round: 1 ch, [dc2tog,] 6 times. Sl st into 1st dc. Fasten off and close hole in back of head.

Attach to top of body.

Ears

With yellow and 3 mm hook make 2 chain.

1st round: 6 dc into 2nd chain from hook. Join with a slip st into 1st dc.

2nd round: 1 ch, 2 dc into same stitch as chain, [2 dc into next dc] 5 times. Sl st into 1st dc. (12 dc)

3rd round; 1ch, 2 ch into same stitch as chain, 1 dc into next dc, [2 dc into next dc, 1 dc into next dc] 4 times, sl st into next 2 dc, sl st into 1st dc.

Fasten off.
Sew on to side of head.

Legs

With yellow double knitting and 3mm hook, chain 10.

1st round: 1dc into 2nd chain from hook. 1 dc into next 7 ch, 2dc into last chain. Working other side of foundation chain, work 2 dc into same place as last dcs. 1 dc into next 7 dc, 3 dc into the same chain as 1st dc worked. Sl st into 1st dc. (22dc)

2nd round: 1ch, 1 dc into same stitch as chain, 1dc into next 8 dc, 2 dc into next 2 dc, 1 dc into next 9 dc, 2 dc into 2 dc. Sl st into 1st dc. (26dc)

3rd and 4th round: 1 ch, 1 dc into each stitch to end, sl st into first dc.

5th round: 1 ch, 1 dc into next 7 dc, [dc2tog] 4 times, 1 dc into next 11 dc. Sl st into 1st dc. (22dc)

6th – 13th rounds: Without joining at the end of each round, work in a spiral for 8 rounds.

14th round: 1 dc into next 4 dc, dc2tog, 1 dc into next 9 dc, dc2tog, 1 dc into next 5 dc. (20dc)

15th – 18th rounds: work 4 rounds without shaping.

19th round: [dc2tog, 1 dc into next 3 dc] 4 times. (16 dc)

20th – 23rd rounds: work 4 rounds without shaping.

24th round: [dc2tog, 1 dc into next 2 dc] 4 times. (12 dc)

25th round: work I round without shaping.

Fasten off and stuff.

Sew across the opening to close and attach legs to the base of the body.

Arms

With yellow and 3 mm hook make 2 chain.

1st round: 6 dc into 2nd chain from hook. Join with a slip st into 1st dc.

2nd round: 1 ch, 2 dc into same stitch as chain, [2 dc into next dc] 5 times. Sl st into 1st dc. (12 dc)

3rd round: 1 ch, 2 dc into same stitch as chain, 1 dc into next dc, [2 dc into next dc, 1 dc into next dc] 5 times. Sl st into 1st dc. (18 dc)

4th – 18th rounds: Without joining at the end of each round, work in a spiral for 15 rounds.

19th round: [dc2tog, 1 dc into next 4 dc] 3 times. (15 sts)

20th – 25th rounds: work 6 rounds without shaping.

26th round: [dc2tog, 1 dc into next 3 dc] 3 times. (12 sts)

27th – 28th rounds: work 2 rounds without shaping.

Fasten off and stuff.

Attach to body.

Sew across the opening to close and attach arms to the sides of the body.

Using black embroidery floss, embroider a cute little nose and some eyes.

Tie a generous pink ribbon around her neck and then give her a cuddle – she's so cute.

Baby's First Doll

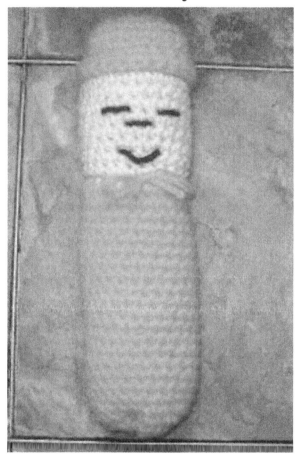

This is a cute and simple "baby's first doll." The photo above is a doll completed by one of my awesome testers, Aurora! She did a great job. This pattern was inspired by a loom-knit doll created by Bev.

Materials:

1 oz. colored WW yarn (for clothes)

small amount of skintone WW yarn (for face)

size H crochet hook

black embroidery floss for features

yarn needle

Foundation(hat) - with clothing color, chain 2. sc 6 in second chain from hook. join. ch.1

round 1 : 2 sc in each sc around. join. ch.1 (12)

round 2 : 2sc in each sc around. join. ch.1 (24)

rounds 3-8 : sc in each sc around. join. ch.1 (24)

round 9 : sc in front loops only - sc in each sc around. join. ch.1(24)

round 10 : sc in each sc around. join. break yarn. (24)

round 11 : join skintone yarn to backloops from round 9 (leaving 10 unattached - the brim of the hat), ch.1. sc in each backloop. join. ch.1(24)

rounds 12-19 : sc in each sc around. join. break yarn. (24)

round 20 : join clothing color. ch. 1. sc in each sc around. join.

ch.1 (24)

rounds 21-40 : sc in each sc around. join. break yarn, leaving a 7"tail. (24)

Stuff doll from the bottom. Thread tail on a yarn needle. Weave through last round, pull tight, tie off. Weave in ends. Embroider on features using thin yarn or embroidery floss. Using a 6" piece of "clothing" yarn and a yarn needle, weave the piece of yarn intothe TOP row of clothing stitches under the head. Pull tight and tie into a bow in the middle to make a "neck".

Baby Soft Sheep Toy

This Baby Soft Sheep Toy is just calling your name. Make this little sheep for your small child. It's made with Simply Soft from Caron worked in rounds.

Crochet HookG/6 or 4 mm hook

Yarn Weight(4) Medium Weight/Worsted Weight and Aran (16-20 stitches to 4 inches)

Toy measures approximately 9 1/2"/24cm tall x 9 1/2"/24cm long

Materials:

- Caron International's Simply Soft (100% Acrylic): 4 oz (A), 4 oz (B)
  - Shown in: #9702 Off White (A) and Caron International's NaturallyCaron.com Country (75% Microdenier Acrylic/25% Merino Wool; 3 oz/85g, 185yds/169m skein): 4 1/2 oz (B) Shown in: #0016 Charcoal (B)
- One size US G-6 (4mm) hook
- Stitch markers
- Polyester fiberfill
- 2 off-white buttons—1"/25mm diameter
- 2 black buttons—2 3/4"/70mm diameter
- Yarn needle

GAUGE

Gauge is not critical for this project.

STITCHES USED

Chain (ch), single crochet (sc), slip stitch (sl st)

SPECIAL STITCHES

double-loop-st: Wrap yarn around index finger twice and hold behind work, insert hook into indicated stitch and between the yarn wraps and your finger, remove your finger from wraps and draw wraps through stitch (leaving part of each wrap on other side of fabric to form loops), yarn over and draw through all loops on hook. Note: Loops form on side of fabric that is facing away from you.

double-loop-st2tog: [Wrap yarn around index finger twice, insert hook into next stitch and between the yarn wraps and your finger, remove your finger from the wraps and wraps through stitch (leaving part of each wrap on other side of fabric to form loops)] twice, yarn over and draw through all loops on hook.

sc2tog: Single crochet 2 together – Insert hook in next stitch, yarn over and pull up a loop, (2 loops on hook), insert hook in next stitch, yarn over and draw up a loop, yarn over and draw through all 3 loops on hook.

NOTES

1. Stuff sheep as work progresses, unless otherwise instructed.

2. Pieces are worked in continuous rounds; do not join and do not turn at end of rounds. Place a marker to indicate beginning of round and move marker up as work progresses.

3. Work tightly so stuffing won't show between stitches.

BODY

With A, ch 2.

Round 1: Work 6 sc in 2nd ch from hook—6 sc. Place a marker for beginning of round. Move marker up as work progresses.

Round 2: Work 2 double-loop-sts in each st around—12 sts.

Round 3: [Double-loop-st in next st, 2 double-loop-sts in next st] 6 times—18 sts.

Round 4: [Double-loop-st in next 2 sts, 2 double-loop-sts in next st] 6 times—24 sts.

Round 5: [Double-loop-st in next 3 sts, 2 double-loop-sts in next st] 6 times—30 sts.

Round 6: [Double-loop-st in next 4 sts, 2 double-loop-sts in next st] 6 times—36 sts.

Round 7: [Double-loop-st in next 5 sts, 2 double-loop-sts in next st] 6 times—42 sts.

Round 8: [Double-loop-st in next 6 sts, 2 double-loop-sts in next st] 6 times—48 sts.

Rounds 9–25: Double-loop-st in each st around.

Round 26: [Double-loop-st in next 6 sts, double-loop-st2tog] 6 times—42 sts.

Round 27: [Double-loop-st in next 5 sts, double-loop-st2tog] 6 times—36 sts.

Round 28: [Double-loop-st in next 4 sts, double-loop-st2tog] 6 times—30 sts.

Round 29: [Double-loop-st in next 3 sts, double-loop-st2tog] 6 times—24 sts.

Round 30: [Double-loop-st in next 2 sts, double-loop-st2tog] 6 times—18 sts.

Round 31: [Double-loop-st in next st, double-loop-st2tog] 6 times—12 sts.

Round 32: [Double-loop-st2tog] 6 times—6 sts.

Fasten off, leaving a long tail. Complete stuffing body. Use tail to sew opening closed.

HEAD

With B, ch 2.

Round 1: Work 6 sc in 2nd ch from hook—6 sc. Place a marker for beginning of round. Move marker up as work progresses.

Round 2: 2 sc in each sc around—12 sc.

Round 3: [Sc in next sc, 2 sc in next sc] 6 times—18 sc.

Round 4: [2 sc in next sc, sc in next 2 sc] 6 times—24 sc.

Round 5: [Sc in next 3 sc, 2 sc in next sc] 6 times—30 sc.

Round 6: [Sc in next 4 sc, 2 sc in next sc] 6 times—36 sc.

Rounds 7 and 8: Sc in each sc around.

Round 9: [Sc in next 5 sc, 2 sc in next sc] 6 times—42 sc.

Rounds 10–19: Sc in each sc around.

Round 20: [Sc in next 3 sc, 2 sc in next sc, sc in next 3 sc] 6 times—48 sc.

Round 21: [Sc in next 7 sc, 2 sc in next sc] 6 times—54 sc.

Round 22: Sc in each sc around.

Round 23: [Sc in next 7 sc, sc2tog] 6 times—48 sts.

Round 24: [Sc in next 3 sts, sc2tog, sc in next 3 sc] 6 times—42 sts.

Round 25: [Sc in next 5 sts, sc2tog] 6 times—36 sts.

Round 26: [Sc in next 2 sts, sc2tog, sc in next 2 sc] 6 times—30 sts.

Round 27: [Sc in next 3 sts, sc2tog] 6 times—24 sts.

Round 28: [Sc in next 2 sts, sc2tog] 6 times—18 sts.

Round 29: [Sc in next st, sc2tog] 6 times—12 sts.

Round 30: [Sc2tog] 6 times—6 sts.

Round 31: [Sk next st, sl st in next st] 3 times—3 sts.

Fasten off.

FLEECE ON TOP OF HEAD

With A, ch 2.

Rounds 1–5: Work Rounds 1–5 of body—30 sc.

Round 6: [Double-loop-st in next 4 sc, 2 double-loop-sts in next st] 4 times; in the following, work double-loop st, but wrap yarn around two fingers instead of one (for longer loops), [double-loop-st in next 4 sc, 2 double-loop-sts in next sc] twice—36 sts.

Fasten off, leaving a long tail for sewing.

LEG (make 4)

With B, ch 2.

Rounds 1–6: Work Rounds 1–6 of head—36 sc.

Round 7: Working in front loops only, sc in each sc around.

Rounds 8 and 9: Sc in each sc around.

Round 10: [Sc in next 5 sc, sc2tog, sc in next 5 sc] 3 times—33 sts.

Round 11: [Sc in next 9 sts, sc2tog] 3 times—30 sts.

Round 12: [Sc in next 4 sts, sc2tog, sc in next 4 sts] 3 times—27 sts.

Round 13: [Sc in next 7 sts, sc2tog] 3 times—24 sts.

Round 14: [Sc in next 3 sts, sc2tog, sc in next 3 sts] 3 times—21 sts.

Rounds 15–24: Sc in each st around.

Fasten off, leaving a long tail for sewing.

EAR (make 2)

Note: Do not stuff ears.

With B, ch 2.

Round 1: Work 6 sc in 2nd ch from hook.

Round 2: Sc in each sc around.

Round 3: [Sc in next sc, 2 sc in next sc] 3 times—9 sc.

Round 4: [Sc in next 2 sc, 2 sc in next sc] 3 times—12 sc.

Round 5: [Sc in next 3 sc, 2 sc in next sc] 3 times—15 sc.

Round 6–12: Sc in each sc around.

Round 13: [Sc in next 3 sc, sc2tog] 3 times—12 sts.

Round 14: [Sc in next 2 sts, sc2tog] 3 times—9 sts.

Round 15: Flatten piece and work through both thicknesses, sc evenly across to seam.

Fasten off, leaving a long tail for sewing.

TAIL

With A, ch 2.

Rounds 1–3: Work Rounds 1–3 of body—18 sts.

Rounds 4–6: Double-loop-st in each st around.

Fasten off, leaving a long tail for sewing.

FINISHING

Sew legs to lower side of body. Stack black buttons on top of white buttons and sew to head. Sew hair to top of head, placing longer loops in front for bangs. Sew ears to top of head. Sew head to front of body. Sew tail to back of sheep, near top of body.

Using yarn needle, weave in all ends.

Totoro

Abbreviations:

st = stitch

sc = single crochet

2tog = 2 stitches together

ch1 = chain one

sl st = slip stitch

f/o = finish off

What I used to make Totoro:

grey worsted weight yarn medium #4

cream colored or off-white worsted weight yarn medium #4

9mm black safety eyes

3.75mm hook

Pieces of Felt

yarn needle

hot glue

Magic ring:

Parts of this amigurumi begin with a magic ring. I have 2 short video tutorials that will show you 2 different methods of making a magic ring. Use the one that is easiest for you. View 1st method and 2nd method.

How to read the rows:

Add a maker at the end of row 2 and move that marker each time you finish a row. Each row has a sequence. Example: 1sc then 2sc in next st means repeat that sequence 1sc then 2sc in next st followed by 1sc then 2sc in next st over and over to the end of that row. When you land on the marker you should be putting in 2sc. If it is a decreasing row then you should be crocheting 2tog when you land on the marker. The number inside the parentheses (~) is the number of stitches you should have at the end of that particular row.

Body: with grey yarn

1) magic circle with 6sc (6)

2) 2sc in each st (12)

3) 1sc then 2sc in next st (18)

4) 1sc in next 2st then 2sc in next st (24)

5) 3sc in first 2st then 1sc in next 10st (32)

6-12) 1sc in each st for 7 rows

13) 1sc in next 3st then 2sc in next st (40)

14) 1sc in each st

15) 1sc in next 7st then 2sc in next st (45)

16-22) 1sc in each st for 7 rows

23) 1sc in next 7st then 2tog (40)

24) 1sc in each st

25) 1sc in next 3st then 2tog (32)

26) 1sc in each st

27) 1sc in next 6st then 2tog (28)

start stuffing doll and shape as you stuff

28) 1sc in next 5st then 2tog (24)

29) 1sc in next 4st then 2tog (20)

30) BLO 1sc in next 3st then 2tog (16)

stuff some more. It will take lots of stuffing and push stuffing towards the sides of the body closer to the bottom of Totoro to make his shape more fat at the bottom. It's always a good idea to keep a picture of the actual character to refer to as you stuff and shape

31) 1sc in next 2st then 2tog (12)

32) 2tog 6 times then f/o. Use a yarn needle to close up any remaining gap then hide yarn tail inside body.

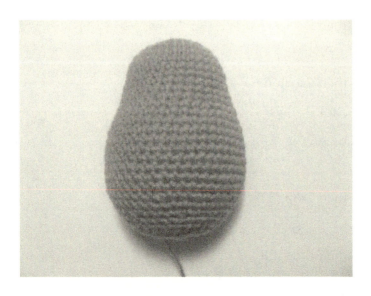

Tummy: with off white or cream color yarn

1) magic circle with 6sc (6)

2) 2sc in each st (12)

3) 1sc in next st, 2sc in next st (18)

4) 1sc in next 2st, 2sc in next st (24)

5) 1sc in next 3st, 2sc in next st (30)

6) 1sc in next 4st, 2sc in next st (36)

7) 1sc in next 5st, 2sc in next st (42)

8) 1sc in each st

sl st into next st and f/o leaving long tail for sewing.

Use a yarn needle and grey yarn to put in the markings in as pictured. Sew piece to body when done. The top edge of the tummy should be sewn at the top edge of the 13th row of Totoro's body. Hide yarn tails in body

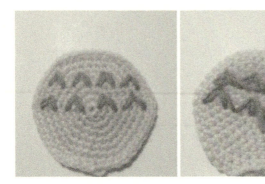

ARMS: with grey yarn

1) magic circle with 6sc (6)

2) 2sc in each st (12)

3) 1sc in next 5st then 2sc in next st (14)

4-8) 1sc in each for 5 rows

9) 1sc in next 5st then 2tog (12)

10-11) 1sc in each for 2 rows

12) ch1 and turn, 1sc in next 6st

f/o leaving long tail for sewing. Lightly stuff lower part of arm and sew the top of the arm to the top of the 13th row of Totoro's body. Hide yarn tails in body.

EARS: with grey yarn

1) magic circle with 6sc (6)

2) 1sc in each st

3) 2sc in each st (12)

4-7) 1sc in each st for 4 rows

8) 2tog 6 times (6)

stuff and shape

9-10) 1sc in each for 2 rows

sl st into next st and f/o leaving long tail for sewing. It is easier to pin the ears in place then sew them in once you are happy with the placement. Hide yarn tails in body

Tail: with grey yarn

1) magic circle with 6sc (6)

2) 2sc in each st (12)

3) 1sc in each st

4) 1sc in next st, 2sc in next st (18)

5) 1sc in each st

6) 1sc in next 2st, 2sc in next st (24)

7) 1sc in each st

8) 1sc in next 2st then 2tog (18)

9) 1sc in each st

sl st into next st and f/o leaving long tail for sewing.

It is easier to partially sew the tail in place then stuff. Finish sewing tail on then hide yarn tail in body

Eyes, Nose and Mouth:

I found a penny a great template for the white parts of the eyes. Place a penny over white felt, trace and then cut. Fold circle in half and snip a tiny slit with scissors. Push a 9mm black safety eye through the slit and then place the stem of the safety eye in between the 7th and 8th row. If you are happy with the spacing and placement then hot glue in place. I found it easier to dab some hot glue on the stem of the eye first, push into head then carefully hot glue the felt down.

With black yarn go through the side of the head as shown, whip stitch a nose in, put a small stitch in for the mouth then carry your yarn back out through the same hole you went into on the side of the head, knot the 2 yarn tails off and hide them inside the body

Amigurumi Duck - A Crochet Pattern

Materials:

- Size 4 worsted weight yarn (100g of white or yellow yarn for the body, 25g orange)

- 3.5 mm crochet hook (these are my favorite to use!)

- 15mm safety eyes

- Black crochet/embroidery thread for eyelashes/small amount of choice color for bow   (optional)

- Scissors

- Tapestry needle (these work wonders for amigurumi with their bent tips)

- Stuffing (Poly-Fil and Morning Glory are my top favorites!)

- Stitch markers

US Abbreviations:

MC- Magic circle

SC- Single crochet

SC INC- Single crochet increase

INV DEC- Invisible decrease

DC- Double crochet

*Slowly stuff as you go, you want it to be firm but not stretched. You will be working in the round, I like using a stitch marker at the beginning of each round.

Legs and Body-

Make 2: Using orange

Round 1: Create a magic circle with 6 SC

Round 2: SC INC in each stitch (12 SC)

Round 3: SC in the first stitch, SC INC in the next stitch, repeat around (18 SC)

Round 4: SC in the first 2 stitches, SC INC in the next stitch, repeat around (24 SC)

Round 5: SC in the first 3 stitches, SC INC in the next stitch, repeat around (30 SC)

Round 6: SC around in the back loops only (30 SC)

Rounds 7-8: SC around (30 SC)

Round 9: SC in the first 9 stitches, INV DEC 6 times, SC in the last 9 stitches (24 SC)

Round 10: SC in the first 6 stitches, INV DEC 6 times, SC in the last 6 stitches (18 SC)

Rounds 11-22: SC around (18 SC)

Fasten off (When you finish the 2nd leg do not fasten. At the end of Round 22 on the 2nd leg, complete a SC in each of the next 6 stitches, this will line up your legs to be straight when we join. Round 23 joins the legs together and starts the body.)

Round 23: Chain 3 and attach to the first leg with a SC (be sure both feet are facing the same direction), SC in the remaining stitches around the leg, when you reach the chain make a SC across each of the 3 chains, SC in the remaining stitches of the next leg and SC across each of the 3 chains (42 SC) This completes your join and is where your next round will start.

Round 24. SC in the first 6 stitches, SC INC in the next, repeat around (48 SC) Change to body color

Round 25: SC around (48 SC)

Round 26: SC in the first 7 stitches, SC INC in the next, repeat around (54 SC)

Rounds 27-38: SC around (54 SC)

Round 39: SC in the first 7 stitches, INV DEC in the next, repeat around (48 SC)

Round 40: SC around (48 SC)

Round 41: SC in the first 6 stitches, INV DEC in the next, repeat around (42 SC)

Round 42: SC around (42 SC)

Round 43: SC in the first 5 stitches, INV DEC in the next, repeat around (36 SC)

Round 44: SC around (36 SC)

Round 45: SC in the first 4 stitches, INV DEC in the next, repeat around (30 SC)

Rounds 46-47: SC around (30 SC)

Fasten off and leave a long tail for sewing

Head-

NOTE: This head will be worked from the top down, meaning the first few rounds will be the top of the head and our closing rounds at the end will be the bottom of our head.

Round 1: Create a magic circle with 6 SC

Round 2: SC INC in each stitch around (12 SC)

Round 3: SC in the first st, SC INC in the next, repeat around (18 SC)

Round 4: SC in the first 2 stitches, SC INC in the next, repeat around (24 SC)

Round 5: SC in the first 3 stitches, SC INC in the next, repeat around (30 SC)

Round 6: SC in the first 4 stitches, SC INC in the next, repeat around (36 SC)

Round 7: SC in the first 5 stitches, SC INC in the next, repeat around (42 SC)

Round 8: SC in the first 6 stitches, SC INC in the next, repeat around (48 SC)

Round 9: SC in the first 7 stitches, SC INC in the next, repeat around (54 SC)

Rounds 10: SC in the first 8 stitches, SC INC in the next, repeat around (60 SC)

Rounds 11-20: SC around (60 SC)

NOTE: Here is where we will attach the safety eyes. Place them 6 stitches apart between rounds 15-17 (If you would like eyelashes you will want to sew them on before securing your safety eyes)

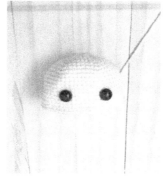

Round 21: SC in the first 8 stitches, INV DEC in the next, repeat around (54 SC)

Round 22: SC in the first 7 stitches, INV DEC in the next, repeat around (48 SC)

Round 23: SC in the first 6 stitches, INV DEC in the next, repeat around (42 SC)

Round 24: SC in the first 5 stitches, INV DEC in the next, repeat around (36 SC)

Round 25: SC in the first 4 stitches, INV DEC in the next, repeat around (30 SC)

Round 26: SC in the first 3 stitches, INV DEC in the next, repeat around (24 SC)

*Continue to stuff the head firmly

Round 27: SC in the first 2 stitches, INV DEC in the next, repeat around (18 SC)

Round 28: SC in the first stitch, INV DEC in the next, repeat around (12 SC)

Round 29: INV DEC around (6 SC)

Fasten off and sew remaining part closed, weave in your end

Beak-

With orange

Round 1: Create a magic circle with 6 SC

Round 2: SC INC in each stitch around (12 SC)

Round 3: SC in the first stitch, SC INC in the next, repeat around (18 SC)

Rounds 4-7: SC around (18 SC)

Fasten off leaving a long tail for sewing

Sew centered between the eyes, stuffing lightly. Options: you can flatten the beak to make a more rectangular bill (example on the white duck) or leave as a circle for a rounded beak (as on the yellow duck).

Wings-

Make 2

Round 1: Create a magic circle with 6 SC

Round 2: SC INC in each stitch around (12 SC)

Round 3: SC in the first stitch, SC INC in the next, repeat around (18 SC)

Round 4: SC in the first 2 stitches, SC INC in the next, repeat around (24 SC)

Round 5: SC in the first 3 stitches, SC INC in the next, repeat around (30 SC)

Rounds 6-8: SC around (30 SC)

Round 9: SC in the first 3 stitches, INV DEC in the next, repeat around (24 SC)

Rounds 10-12: SC around (24 SC)

Round 13: SC in the first 2 stitches, INV DEC in the next, repeat around (18 SC)

Rounds 14-22: SC around (18 SC)

At the end of round 22 pinch the wing flat and make 8 SC across the top to close, fasten off and leave a long tail to sew onto the body

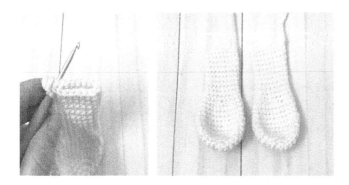

Tail-

Round 1: Create a magic circle with 6 SC

Round 2: SC INC in each stitch around (12 SC)

Rounds 3-4: SC around (12 SC)

Round 5: SC in the first stitch, SC INC in the next, repeat around (18 SC)

Round 6: SC around (18 SC)

Round 7: SC in the first 6 stitches, SC INC in the next 6 stitches, SC in each of the last 6 stitches (24 SC)

Round 8: SC around (24 SC)

Round 9: *SC in the first 6 stitches, SC INC in the next 3 stitches*, repeat from * one more time, SC in the last 6 stitches (30 SC)

Round 10: SC around (30 SC)

Round 11: SC in the first 6 stitches, SC INC in the next 3 stitches, SC in the next 12 stiches, SC INC in the next 3 stitches, SC in the last 6 stitches (36 SC)

Fasten off leaving a long tail for sewing

Attaching everything together-

Sew the head onto the body, making sure to have the facial features centered. Add extra stuffing as you go to keep it firm and less wobbly.

Next sew the wings onto the body centered with the head at round 46. Sew the tail centered on the back of the body, lightly stuffing as you go.

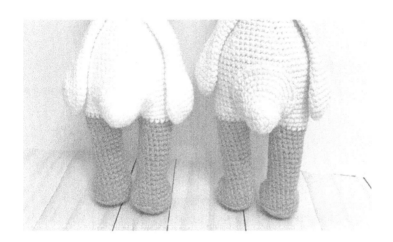

Optional Bow-

Working in a magic circle make 7 DCs, slip stitch, 7 DCs, and slip stitch again, pull your string tight and wrap it around the middle of the bow 4 times.

Tie/secure in the back and cut your string leaving a long section to sew with. Sew onto your favorite side of the head!

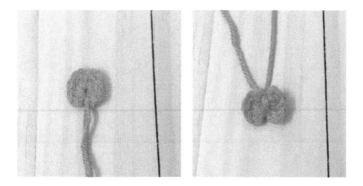

Your duck is complete! I hope you have enjoyed making this pattern.

Let me know if you have any questions with this pattern or any of my other patterns, I would be happy to help.

Baby Rattles

Looking for a last minute baby shower gift? These baby crochet patterns are so fun to make and they're easy too. Baby will love playing with these rattles as they love noises.

Measurements: Approx 4 (6½-14) ins [10 (16.5-35.5) cm] long x 3 ins [7.5 cm] in diameter.

Materials:

- Bernat® Baby Cakes (100 g / 3.5 oz; 185 m / 203 yds)

MEDIUM OR LARGE - Dual or Caterpillar Rattles

- A: (43205 Shamrock) or (43201 Honey Dew) 1 ball
- B: (43414 Tickled Pink) or (43425 Sea shell) 1 ball

SMALL - Egg Rattle

- A: (43205 Shamrock) or (43414 Tickled Pink) 1 ball
- B: (43007 Ice Cream) 1 ball
- Size 4 mm (U.S G or 6) crochet hook or size needed to obtain gauge. Stuffing. Plastic cat rattle approx 1¾ ins [4.5 cm] in diameter.

Gauge

21 sc and 22 rows = 4 ins [10 cm].

Instructions:

The instructions are written for Egg Rattle. If changes are necessary for Dual Rattle or Caterpillar Rattle the instructions will be written thus ( ).

Note: Join all rnds with sl st to first sc.

Body: With B, ch 2.

1st rnd: 6 sc in 2nd ch from hook. Join.

2nd rnd: Ch 1. 2 sc in each sc around. Join. 12 sc.

3rd rnd: Ch 1. (2 sc in next sc. 1 sc in next sc) 6 times. Join. 18 sc.

4th rnd: Ch 1. (2 sc in next sc. 1 sc in each of next 2 sc) 6 times. 24 sc.

5th rnd: Ch 1. (2 sc in next sc. 1 sc in each of next 3 sc) 6 times. Join. 30 sc.

6th rnd: Ch 1. (2 sc in next sc. 1 sc in each of next 4 sc) 6 times. Join

50

A. 36 sc.

**7th rnd: With A, ch 1. 1 sc in each sc around. Join.

Rep last rnd 4 times more, then with B, rep last rnd 5 times more.**

Rep from ** to ** 0 (1-4) time(s) more. Break A.

Top shaping: 1st rnd: With B, ch 1. (Sc2tog. 1 sc in each of next 4 sc) 6 times. Join. 30 sts.

2nd and alt rnds: Ch 1. 1 sc in each st around. Join.

3rd rnd: Ch 1. (Sc2tog. 1 sc in each of next 3 sc) 6 times. Join. 24 sts.

5th rnd: Ch 1. (Sc2tog. 1 sc in each of next 2 sc) 6 times. Join. 18 sts.

Wrap stuffing around cat rattle and place in Rattle.

7th rnd: Ch 1. (Sc2tog. 1 sc in next st) 6 times. Join. 12 sts.

8th rnd: Ch 1. (Sc2tog) 6 times. 6 sts. Fasten off. Thread end onto tapestry needle and draw tightly through rem sts.

Thread coordinating color through (Dual Rattle-Caterpillar Rattle) to create (2-5) lumps. Pull tightly. Fasten securely.

Hedgehog Taggie Baby Toy

This project took me a while to figure out. My first try came out a little lopsided, but attempt number two came out much better, so that's what I'm teaching you today. Let's get started!

I'm trying a bit of a pictorial this time around, since I found it a bit hard to explain (to myself) what I did.

You'll need yarn, of course, and the usual crocheting implements. You'll also need the ribbon for the tags. For the stuffing, I chose to use a 1/2" cotton piping which I magically found in my stash. I imagine regular ol' polyfill should also work, but this tutorial assumes you're using piping. I think I bought mine at JoAnn's, but who knows really.

The ribbon pieces should be cut a bit longer than twice the length of the desired tag, think of it as a seam allowance. So, if your tag is 1 inch, then you should cut the ribbon to be maybe 3 inches. Ok, off to the pictures! And don't worry, the entire pattern is down below.

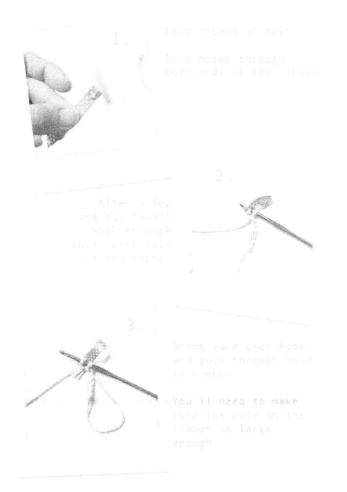

1. Fold ribbon in half.

Poke holes through both ends of the ribbon.

2.

After a few chains, insert hook through ribbon with fold to the right.

3.

Bring yarn over hook, and pull through hold to ribbon.

You'll need to make sure the hole in the ribbon is large enough.

Complete the chain
by pulling yarn
through loop on
hook.

Chain 3.

Work next piece of
ribbon into chain.

Continue working
chains and adding
the remaining
ribbon pieces.

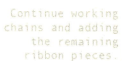

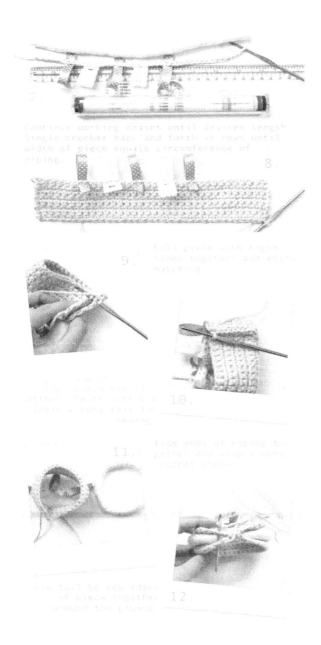

And ta da! There you have it! No, not really. All you have right now is a ring with no head, but it's a lovely ring.

57

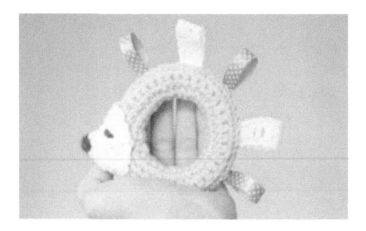

Here's the full pattern:

SUPPLIES:

Lily Sugar'n Cream Cotton yarn in white, brown, and color of choice

Size F crochet hook

Yarn needle

Scissors

Sharp Crochet Hook or pin for poking holes in the ribbon

5 pieces of ribbon for the tags

9 inches of 1/2" cotton piping

small amount of fiberfill (optional)

INSTRUCTIONS:

1. Chain 6.

2. *Work 1st piece of folded ribbon onto chain. Chain 3.* Repeat until all 5 pieces of ribbon are worked onto chain.

3. Continue chain until total number of chains is 36. Turn. (36 sts)

(Note: The number of stitches will depend on the length of your piping and how big you want the ring to be.)

4. Row 1 – 8: SC into second chain from hook. Work 1 SC in each stitch across. Chain 1. Turn. (36 sts)

(Note: I used 8 rows, but the number of rows will vary depending on your gauge and size of piping. The crocheted piece needs to wrap around the piping, so you'll need to check as you go.)

5. Fold piece cross-wise with right sides facing each other, wrong sides facing out. Align the rough edges.

6. Slip stitch through both edges/ends across the width of the piece.

7. Fasten off. Cut yarn but leave a very long tail. The tail will be used to close the seam around, so make sure you leave enough yarn to get you home.

8. Tape the ends of the piping together to form a ring.

9. Put the piping ring around the outside of the crochet piece. The wrong side of the crochet piece should be touching the piping.

10. Use the yarn tail to whip stitch the crochet seams together, and enclose the piping. It may be helpful to count your stitches before you start so they line up correctly. You'll be stitching through the ribbon tags, with the ribbon allowance being tucked into the piece.

11. Fasten off, and weave in ends.

HEAD:

Round 1. With white yarn, SC 4 into a magic circle.

Round 2. *SC 1 in next stitch, sc 2 in next stitch.* Repeat from *. (6 sts)

Round 3. Work 2 SC into each of next 3 sts. SC 1 in each of remaining 3 sts. (9 sts)

Round 4. Work 2 SC into each of next 3 sts. SC 1 in each of remaining 6 sts. (12 sts)

Round 5. Work 2 SC into each of next 3 sts. SC 1 in each of remaining 9 sts. (15 sts)

Round 6. Work 2 SC into each of next 3 sts. SC 1 in each of remaining 12 sts. (18 sts)

Fasten off. Cut yarn, leaving a long tail for sewing.

The head is a lopsided cone, and should be positioned with the nose upwards. Use the brown yarn to embroider a nose where the magic circle is. Add eyes with the yarn, or use safety eyes.

Using the white yarn tail, attach the head to the ring where the joining seam is. Optionally, you can stuff the head with a bit of fiberfill to give your hedgehog some puffy cheeks.

Made in the USA
Monee, IL
21 May 2021